DAVID SCLAR

WORKPLACE STRATEGIES
FOR
TECHNOLOGY LAWYERS

36 Practical Tips on
**HOW TO COMMUNICATE MORE EFFECTIVELY,
WORK MORE EFFICIENTLY, *and* GIVE BETTER ADVICE**
as In-House Counsel at a Tech Company

Cover and text design by Brian Phillips Design.

ISBN: 979-8-59714-186-2

First Edition

THOUGHTS ABOUT THE BOOK

"This is so much more than a 'what they don't teach you in law school' book. The book lays out nearly every essential, non-intuitive skill needed to effectively provide legal advice and service tech companies. Most notably, it focuses on how to be a valued partner—not a cost center—and demystifies one of the most important and least understood industries in the world. Concise, well organized, easy-to-understand and at times funny, this book is a gem for any lawyer who wishes to earn the respect of their business colleagues and assist in achieving company goals."

—*Natasha Kohne, Partner at Akin Gump and co-head of the cybersecurity, privacy, and data protection practice*

"David Sclar provides readers with a veritable guide on what it takes to be an effective in-house attorney for tech companies, offering nuts-and-bolts practical advice on day-to-day life and issues that such attorneys are likely to encounter. This is a must-read for any attorney seeking to move in-house with a technology company: it will open your eyes and help you understand exactly what you will be getting yourself into. Perhaps more importantly, it will help you decide if such a role is the right fit for your personality and career."

—*Darin Morgan, Partner and Managing Partner, Philadelphia at Major, Lindsey & Africa*

"Insightful guidance from an experienced and battle-tested in-house tech lawyer. Not only is this book a must-read for new in-house tech counsel—it's also a reminder to veteran in-house counsel in all fields and their law firm advisers. David Sclar offers simple, straightforward practical advice on how lawyers can partner with their business folks to find valued solutions. His advice about understanding context and finding closure are necessary ingredients in establishing a successful relationship with business partners."

—*Thora Johnson, Partner at Venable*

"Workplace Strategies for Technology Lawyers provides in-house technology lawyers a vast array of tools to provide accurate and timely solutions to their clients. It also makes the important, and often overlooked, point that while fundamental legal skills are table stakes, cultural fit and business acumen are mandatory to be a consummate in-house practitioner. Ultimately, the book provides powerful and useful tools that technology lawyers—really all lawyers—will enjoy and benefit from."

—*Troy Cahill, General Counsel and Corporate Secretary at LaserShip, Inc.*

CONTENTS

INTRODUCTION

I am a tech company lawyer. Maybe you are or will be too. Or maybe you know one who would appreciate some on-the-ground advice. I decided to write this book because I've had the opportunity to learn lessons firsthand that I want to share with others.

I learned those lessons:

- As outside counsel to tech companies at BigLaw firms Ropes & Gray and Cooley;

- At Rally Health, where I joined a rapidly growing startup as their second lawyer and Chief Privacy Officer. I helped the company grow through "Unicorn" status, acquisition by Optum/UnitedHealthcare, and integration with related business lines; and

- As Healthcare Compliance and Privacy Officer at WW International (formerly Weight Watchers),[1] where I am currently helping WW emphasize tech-focused initiatives for its proven weight loss program.

A lack of training for tech company lawyers

Looking back, I realize I could only gain a limited understanding of what I was embarking upon when I began working as a tech company lawyer or when I went in house in 2014. I don't think many lawyers working at large law firms or government jobs would know what to expect. And that's a problem. Tech companies are fast paced and need lawyers who understand what will be expected of them, fit culturally, and know how to hit the ground running. Lawyers need to know what they're getting into, whether the job is right for them, and what it takes to succeed.

There are unique challenges for tech lawyers, who must provide legal counsel for companies using unprecedented technology to develop products and services faster than regulators can imagine them. These challenges extend to all companies with a technology element, whether as a new business line or through SaaS, cloud hosting, or other technology vendors. Throughout the book, I will refer to tech

---

1   All views in this book are my own.

companies specifically, but the advice really applies to all companies with a substantial tech component.

This is a book for tech company lawyers, present and future, and those who work with them

As far as I can tell, the only way to know what it takes to be a tech company lawyer is to be a tech company lawyer. That kind of on-the-job training is not what most lawyers prepared for in law school. So, this book seeks to make life a little easier for tech company lawyers looking to:

- do their job well;
- reduce friction in their work;
- increase the uptake of their legal advice; and
- broaden their skill set.

This is also a book for:

- Law firm lawyers looking to join a tech company;
- Law firm lawyers wanting to better understand and deliver for their tech company clients;
- Law students considering legal careers at tech companies;
- Tech companies looking to hire a lawyer with the right skill set;

- Non-legal colleagues at tech companies seeking a better understanding of how to work with the legal department; and

- Friends and family who want to understand what the role requires.

Ultimately, there's no substitute for experience. But this book can give you a running start.

Structure of the book: 36 Tips of short, practical advice grouped into 8 Sections

The structure of this book is 36 Tips grouped into 8 Sections covering key aspects of the job. These cover how to:

- Give good, practical advice;

- Think of good advice in the first place;

- Avoid making mistakes;

- Keep pace and stay above water;

- Be an expert communicator—an essential skill at tech companies;

- Work with other teams;

- Know the product, company, industry, customers, and users well;

- Navigate office life during coronavirus and after; and much more.

This is not a book about the substance of the law. To use language familiar to lawyers and law students, fundamental legal skills are necessary, but not sufficient. It's also not a book on the latest technologies or how to get the job. This is a book to help you do the job, and do it well. If I've done my job well, not only will you be glad you read this book, but so will your present or future tech company colleagues.

GIVING GOOD, PRACTICAL ADVICE

As this book will demonstrate, there are multiple aspects to being a good tech lawyer, but it all starts with good advice. What does good advice look like? In the tech world, good advice is clear and actionable—so it gets implemented. In this first Section, I will unpack how to give good advice, solve for underlying questions, and prepare for every meeting where your advice will be needed.

Tip #1: Solutions, not issue spotting

A good tech company counsel is a problem solver who not only frames issues but also charts a course of action. If you raise issues, make sure you bring solutions and alternatives.

When you join a tech company, you're in new territory, and spotting the issues takes talent and instinct. You're called upon to analyze products and services where the legal issues are not obvious. You're asked to issue spot quickly and often for diverse matters across the business. The goalposts keep moving as the business evolves. The legal team is likely lean, and you're expected to function independently.

In short, spotting the issues in this environment takes talent, so there may be a temptation to stop at issue spotting and say, "Well, I did my job and I warned the business." But if you stop there, you haven't done your full job. Everyone, from the business to other lawyers, will look to you help solve the problems you raise. This requires going further than you might have at a law firm and asking yourself how things could be different. Maybe there's a compromise approach? Could the legal issue be solved with: phrasing things a bit differently, working with a vendor to change how data is exchanged, or getting a representation in a contract to protect the company? Does everything have to be addressed now or could it be triaged?

Use your creativity—this is a perk of the job!—and your judgment to offer solutions. Even if they aren't adopted, they will advance the discussion. If you stop at issue spotting, everyone will keep looking to you for business-advancing solutions—until they stop because they aren't getting what they need.

Tip #2: Solve for the underlying question

When you're at a law firm, your client is often a lawyer. They aren't perfect, but lawyers can generally put their finger on the legal issues they need help with.

At a tech company, in-house "clients" (i.e. colleagues) probably have little idea what legal issues are in play. It's your job to recognize the legal issues and solve for them. The work required to fully address a matter may be very different than it looks on its face. It takes judgment and confidence to ask the right questions, tease out the underlying issues, and start solving them.

Sometimes the missing underlying issues aren't even legal, or they concern *different* legal issues than what a surface-level analysis would suggest. For example, a product manager may ask, "Can we share this user data with our customer?", where "customer" refers to a business that pays for your product or service. However, the real business issue may be that the customer wants to use the data to offer users rewards that are not part of the product you're selling. That's a potential business issue and raises legal questions about those customer-provided rewards that go beyond data sharing.

Why didn't the product manager just ask about supporting customer-specific rewards schemes? Never forget that business teams have bosses and budgets. Both create a sense of pressure and immediacy that can influence whether to wrestle with a customer demand or start working on it.

A STORY OF SOLVING FOR THE "QUESTIONS BEHIND THE QUESTION"

A terrific parable captures what separates average tech company counsel from great counsel: the ability to understand what's really being asked, use judgment, and drive towards solutions. As told by author Benjamin Hardy,[1] a father is deciding which of his two sons to pass his farm down to. He asks both of his sons to find out from Cibi's farm if any cows are for sale. The older son reports back that Cibi has six cows for sale. The younger son is a problem solver, and his answer says everything about good counsel:

"Father, Cibi has six cows for sale. Each cow will cost 2,000 rupees. If we are thinking about buying more than six cows, Cibi said he would be willing to reduce the price 100 rupees. Cibi also said they are getting special jersey cows next week if we aren't in a hurry, it may be good to wait. However, if we need the cows urgently, Cibi said he could deliver the cows tomorrow."

This answer doesn't just solve for the simple question being asked—it also solves for the implied questions (the "questions behind the question") and demonstrates a thoughtfulness about the long-term wellbeing of the farm. As a result, the father passes down his farm to the younger son. Likewise, solving for the under-lying issues will help earn you results you're seeking—and it will demonstrate your value to the team.

---

1   https://www.businessinsider.com/story-about-a-farmer-shows-what-separates-average-from-successful-2017-10

By all means, be sensitive to these pressures. But for the sake of the business and doing *your* job, make sure to help solve the underlying problem.

Tip #3: Good advice provides: 1) guidance; 2) closure; and 3) wiggle room

Consider guidance, closure, and wiggle room the three-legged stool of good in-house counsel. Failing to factor in any of these three can create a messy situation.

1. **Guidance:** I chose "Giving Good, Practical Advice" as the very first Section in this book for a reason: to be a successful tech company counsel, you simply have to provide solutions. (See Tip #1: "Solutions, not issue spotting.")

2. **Closure:** Closure means ensuring everyone knows next steps. Conveying clear next steps or results assigns responsibility and ensures progress for the business. Failure to convey next steps or results creates confusion, prevents progress, and risks labeling Legal as the department that is holding up the business. I will cover this more in Tip #16: "Always be closing."

3. **Wiggle room:** Allowing yourself some wiggle room might sound controversial or contradictory to the first two "legs" of the stool. It's not. It's self-preservation.

You give counsel with the information you have at a point in time, but new information could come to light next year, month, or even the very next day. The only constant is change—especially at a tech company. The smart way to handle this is to:

> › Make clear what information forms the basis of your conclusions.

> › Feel free to remind the business: "If things change, please let me know so I can give you the best advice possible."

> › If you foresee critical new information that could affect your analysis, call it out.

> › Better yet, anticipate when that new information will become available, remind yourself to revisit the analysis, and affirmatively reach out to the business with updated guidance when you have more information. (See the next Tip for more advice on this subject.)

Tip #4: Work management is essential

Prepare for every meeting. You may be exceptionally smart, but you won't give the most relevant, insightful, best advice unless you prepare. A good analogy here is clerking for a district court versus an appellate court. In-house legal work at a tech company has the pace and robust daily calendar of a district court. It's rare that you'll write a memo or even an email over a page in length. And your calendar will look as choppy as the wood at an axe throwing bar. It's easy to be overwhelmed, so taking an hour or two in the evenings or weekends to prepare what you'll say at each meeting goes a long way.

Other keys to work management include tracking follow-ups and outcomes and making a clean record:

- **Tracking follow-ups and outcomes** means checking whether work gets completed, advice gets implemented, and results are achieved. This helps move things forward and makes sure things get done. (It also helps you personally by ensuring your work on a matter is successful and appreciated at annual reviews.)

- **Making a clean record** means making a written record—e.g., an email or note to self (this doesn't have to be formal)—of what was discussed and decided, what are next steps, and who is responsible for them. This is important because as time passes, you will forget where things landed today. So, by making a clean record you make follow-up more effective and do your future self a favor. (For more tips on making a clean record see Tip #16: "Always be closing.")

PRACTICAL TIPS FOR FOLLOWING UP

- Set a reminder immediately after a meeting or sending an email that will require follow-up. To do so, you can utilize flags and other email system tools—whatever works best for you. My personal favorites are 1) snooze and 2) calendar reminders.

- Snoozing emails allows you to keep your inbox clean and set a time for an email to pop back in. If the matter has been resolved in the interim, you can just file it away or delete it when it returns. Often, the return of the email will be the reminder you need to take the next step.

- Calendar reminders—set to "private" and "available"!— allow you to not only set a reminder for yourself but also include notes, links, and subject lines of relevant emails. Use a different, fun color to distinguish reminders from your meetings.

  Whatever tools you use, take action right away after meetings or sending emails, or at the end of the day when you clear out the day's emails, so you don't forget later!

THINKING OF GOOD ADVICE

It's hard to teach good judgment. My goal here is to give you a running start for making judgment calls at a tech company. If you've ever talked to a consultant about what they do all day, you might get an answer like, "I implement industry-leading practices to solve mission-critical business problems for Fortune 500 companies." Impressive, but not much in the way of a practical roadmap for you to succeed on the job. So, I'll try to be more helpful by breaking down some key skills for seeing the angles.

Tip #5: Ask for context

As you'll note in my table of contents, this is not the only Tip that underscores the need for context to be successful in the job. (See Tip #19: "Context is everything—both receiving and providing" for information on how context enables you to be an expert communicator.) The reason I include it twice is simple: Context *is* everything. When presented with an issue, the context will lead you to good judgment.

When sizing up good advice for a given situation, key contextual clues include:

- **What**: Obviously, make sure you feel like you have full information to understand the situation. If not, ask!

- **Who**: Who is involved? What do you know about them? What are their goals, tendencies, preferences, etc.? Is anyone the best friend of your CEO?

- **When**: Are there deadlines? What is the basis for the deadlines? When did the most recent events happen? Has time passed in between and could things have changed? Is someone waiting and getting frustrated?

- **Where**: Where is the relevant activity taking place? What laws might apply in that country/state? Are multiple countries/states involved?

- **How**: How do they want an answer? In writing? In real-time? In depth? At a high level?

- **Why**: Why does this question even matter to the business? What is at stake? (See Tip #2: "Solve for the underlying question" for more information.)

I could go on, but the point is simple. Context helps you look at a problem from all angles and gets you thinking about solutions—and not just solutions, solutions in context. Now that's good judgment!

USING CONTEXT TO TAKE THE RIGHT APPROACH TO A CHALLENGING QUESTION

Given the fast-paced nature of a tech counsel job, it may be tempting to jump right to legal analysis without first getting the context you need, but that risks building a house on a sand foundation.

An upset user once insisted we send her husband's personal information to a police officer who was conducting a criminal investigation. Various data sharing laws may have exceptions that allow for sharing with law enforcement. It was tempting to start analyzing, perhaps with the expense of outside counsel.

But the first thing we did was talk to the police officer. It turned out he had no interest in investigating what turned out to be a nasty personal dispute but not a criminal matter. With that context, we were able to refocus the conversation and avoid spending time, effort, and money on law enforcement issues.

Tip #6: Use data for decisions

There's one particular type of context that deserves a special callout: Data. In case you hadn't heard, it's the new bacon.

Relevant data can provide important context that can change your entire analysis of an issue. And if the data isn't there, it can often be generated or researched.

Sample data questions include:

- How many users are affected by this issue? How many customers?

- Is this the first time we've had this issue with this customer? What happened last time?

- What is our annual revenue from that customer?

- How many user complaints did we get before we added that new feature? How many since?

- What do users do when they land on that screen? What is their next step?

- What are our competitors' practices in this area?

Not only does data help point you in the right direction, but it also helps you make your case effectively. Data tells a story—about user behavior, issues with product features, revenue, and so on. With data providing crucial context, you can make a far better case for implementing a change than simply concluding "We're at risk."

A better argument explains:

"This product feature has generated 100 negative user contacts in two weeks. Ten of them are from our largest customer. And a regulatory agency fined another company millions of dollars based on similar facts. So, this is a high risk in need of a prioritized fix."

This evidence-based argument uses data to highlight the rationale for addressing the product feature at issue, and gives the team needed context to start building a targeted solution.

Tip #7: Get comfortable managing risk

One of your roles as tech company counsel will be to assess, articulate, and get comfortable with risk. It's inconvenient that many lawyers are risk averse and that highly polished law firm work may obscure some of the hardest decisions around risk.

In its simplest terms, risk is a function of the extent of potential harm and the likelihood of its occurrence. This can be expressed as: **Risk = Probability x Harm**.

This handy equation helps break down most problems that come your way so you can articulate risk to the business. Ultimately, the business will usually make a decision whether to proceed based on your input as well as the potential rewards. Unless there's a high probability of substantial harm, the legal team is unlikely to put their foot down and act as a "blocker." But of course, when an idea crosses the line, it's your job to say so.

Think of risk as an invitation for creativity. You can effectively work to mitigate any level of risk by thinking creatively about both the law and the business initiative and figuring out new approaches to each. This is an opportunity to utilize your role as a problem solver (see Tip #1: "Solutions, not issue spotting"); your knowledge of the product, the business, the industry, customers, and users (see Section VII: "Things You Should Know Well"); and everything you know about context (see Tip #19: "Context is everything—both receiving and providing") or relevant data (see Tip #6: "Use data for decisions"). If this feels like putting pieces of the puzzle together, you're getting a good feel for the job. This can be one of the most enjoyable parts of the job as you help the business iterate an idea so everyone can proceed with confidence.

It is important to think broadly about risk, and about which risks are actually in play. Even if a law isn't necessarily violated, there can be a variety of other risks such as: 1) a lawsuit; 2) invitation of regulatory scrutiny; 3) breach of contract; 4) demands for audits; 5) use of legal concerns as leverage for business demands; 6) loss of customers; and 7) negative media coverage.

Do not limit yourself to legal risk. For one thing, the

business is not especially interested in legal risk for its own sake. They want to know the impact on revenue and how it will affect their "product roadmap" (the schedule for launching new products on time) and their workload (often, engineering workload and often referred to as a "tech lift").

It is far more compelling for you to think about non-legal risks, because these get everyone's attention. For example, if a new regulation may require rebuilding the product, that has potential to blow up the roadmap and cause engineers to spend some weekends rebuilding something instead of designing the something new. There are of course legal reasons to comply with the new regulation, but you will have everyone's attention for non-legal reasons.

Tip #8: The grey area is your friend

Don't be afraid of the grey area. By working at a tech company, you need to apply old laws and regulations to new technologies and situations not contemplated by the drafters. The answer you're looking for may not be directly in the statutory or regulatory language. In the absence of guidance on specifics, your job is to help the business navigate uncertainty.

A trailblazing technology requires flexibility, but there's also opportunity. You can look to the laws and regulations and draw reasonable conclusions about how they would apply to today's products. Think about the policy reasons behind the laws and look for the most recent agency opinions or publications that may be applicable. Be sure to document the company's view, the facts available to you, and the rationale for that view. You can also ask the regulator for guidance on your specific situation, but that's often unnecessary and has trade-offs because it might generate an undesirable opinion. Whatever course you choose, do your diligence and don't look for "loopholes." Get clear on the information you have and make a reasonable decision based on evidence—by extrapolating in the context of a grey area.

Tip #9: Everyone is a safety officer

In his book *Outside the Wire*, former army captain and politician Jason Kander describes how on the army marksmanship range, everyone is a safety officer. In other words, everyone in a training exercise has the authority and the responsibility to shut down the range at any time by calling out "Cease fire! Cease fire!" for safety reasons. Jason says he "often wish[es] we treated lying this way in politics."[2]

Similarly, as a tech company lawyer it helps to remember that everyone is a safety officer for issues affecting the

---

2   Jason Kander, *Outside the Wire: Ten Lessons I've Learned in Everyday Courage* (New York: Grand Central Publishing, 2018.)

business. While you need to do your legal role well, you want to be considered a team player whose role is bigger than knowing the law. One way you play a larger role is by identifying product bugs, miscommunications, deadline confusion, or misaligned priorities. Lawyers by nature are particularly well adapted for catching issues. Of course, no one wants you over their shoulder all the time, but if you spot something that affects colleagues outside of Legal and seems to be slipping through the cracks—such as a customer demand that needs to be remembered and respected—you can win a lot of points with everyone involved and make your own life easier by bringing it up.

Tip #10: Get relevant certifications

I know the bar exam was the last exam you ever wanted to take. I get it. But if there are certifications in a relevant area of law, I suggest you go for it. In a world where Netflix is so compelling after work, it can be hard to motivate yourself to hone your craft. Certifications promise a two-for-one special: You learn new skills and you get a credential for your resume.

I've had the opportunity to get certifications in privacy and security that have augmented my in-house work. My study books became a resource for my day job, and the body of knowledge made me a better lawyer.

There are certifications from industry groups, online degree programs, and Massive Open Online Courses (MOOCs) from resources such as Coursera, and they cover many areas of law and business (from legal specialties to relevant business topics like artificial intelligence, data analytics, and project management). In fact, another added benefit of certifications is they often come with membership in a professional organization such as the International Association of Privacy Professionals (IAPP) and the International Information System Security Certification Consortium ((ISC)^2), which brings opportunities for networking and continued learning.

Finally, certifications tend to teach you foundational principles, and it never hurts to take a "first principles" approach to questions on the job. In describing first principles in an interview,[3] Elon Musk explains: You start with what you know is true (e.g., the cost of battery constituent parts) and you reason how to solve problems around that (e.g., developing a cheaper battery). Certifications teach essential truths in the field that you can use to address any new challenge.

---

3 The interview, conducted by Kevin Rose for innomind.org, can be found here: https://www.youtube.com/watch?v=NV3sBlRgzTI.

AVOIDING DISASTERS

In football, you can often win the game if you don't turn the ball over, and it's especially hard to win if you turn the ball over frequently. Likewise, as a tech company lawyer, if you avoid significant mistakes you'll likely be in good shape. In this Section, I recommend methods for avoiding game-changing mistakes.

Tip #11: Ask yourself: What aren't they telling you?

The easiest way to make a mistake is to not ask the right questions. As I discuss throughout this book, context is everything. If you don't get full information, you won't be able to fully solve the problem.

For example, make sure you understand all deadlines, including the lead time that will be required to complete a given project. Even a change of a few words of legal language can take days, if not weeks, to implement because it has to be coded and subject to Quality Assurance (QA) to make sure it doesn't break the product.

Likewise, make sure all the right teams are involved. The product team asking for your input may not have consulted with security, privacy, account management, engineering, experience design, other product teams, and so on. You'll want to understand who's missing and help bring them in. Otherwise, you could end up doing substantial work on a project that's going to change significantly once other key players find out about it.

Make sure to question vendors especially carefully. Vendor sales and business teams are quick to make promises they sometimes can't keep in order to get a deal done. For example, HIPAA requires certain vendors to sign a Business Associate Agreement (BAA) which obligates the vendor to comply with HIPAA. I've had multiple potential vendors assure my business team they would sign a BAA. There was just one question: Do they actually comply with HIPAA? When asked point blank, they admitted they do not.

So, to avoid trouble, you need to ask questions to get the information you need and involve everyone whose input is needed.

Tip #12: Ask yourself: What don't you know?

On a related note, sometimes clear information is hard to come by. It's no secret that tech companies work with the latest and greatest technology, and it's often hard to understand at a detailed level. Unfortunately, the legal implications often depend on the details, and it's your job to recognize when they are missing and to ask for information to fill in the blanks as needed. Often no one will have the answer, but that's exactly why you ask: so the business can make a plan to find out the details before proceeding.

WHEN TO TRUST PEOPLE

A word about trusting people. You need to know whom to trust and whose explanations require some unpacking. Colleagues at a tech company are under pressure, moving quickly, and ambitious, so mistakes are inevitable.

My suggestion is to collect a series of data points. If your BigLaw partner used to say "If there's one mistake I can't trust anything," that's likely too stringent at a tech company. But if you notice a pattern, take extra care to get the context and details when working with that person.

Tip #13: Make clear what's internal only

Here's a simple but helpful tip: Make clear—**like bolded and upfront**—when information is **internal only**. It happens all the time: business teams forward your candid, and internal-only!, advice to a customer, user, or potential business partner. The result may cost you attorney-client privilege associated with your advice, expose legal issues outside the company, and undermine negotiating leverage by disclosing the company's position. Don't let it happen to you. Likewise, try to anticipate anything others might do with your emails and head it off!

Tip #14: Think all the way through the cascades

It's important to remember that nothing happens in a vacuum. When a business adds a product feature, it will have to be designed and built, tested by QA, reviewed by Security, rolled out to customers, experienced by users, and trained on by customer support who will ultimately field user questions and concerns. Wherever possible, try to think ahead about how a decision will affect other teams. When action in one area of the business burdens another area of the business, you generally can't throw users, customers, or business partners under the bus. So, if something you help build sets back another team or leads to upset customers or users that threaten to lower your Net Promoter Score (NPS, a measure of customer satisfaction), well, look out for the bus.

STAYING ABOVE WATER

At this point, you may be wondering how a tech company counsel manages to do the job. There's no question the pace can be intense. You'll often hear tech companies explain that they're building the airplane while it's flying, or make similar comparisons. This Section recommends how to keep up with the pace and demands of a tech company.

Tip #15: You don't need to "book" everything

You don't need to ace everything the way you would "book" a law school exam. That doesn't mean you should give lazy or incorrect advice, but it does mean you can take a bit of the polish off. Think emails, not memos; colloquial language, not formal; and some element of shooting from the hip while checking your work where necessary.

You also must learn to accept you won't get to everything on your to-do list. You simply have to triage, and that means accepting some things will happen down the road. If you're Type A—amen, I'm with you—it can be difficult to let go, but it's a necessity. Consider it a luxury to always focus on the most important (or at least the most time-sensitive) work.

Tip #16: Always be closing

Closure is your friend. Better yet, closure with a clean record is your best friend. The business teams need to know the outcome of legal reviews so they can take their next steps with confidence. And while you juggle many balls as a tech company lawyer, you need to find a way to put them down.

Bringing closure to matters might sound simple, but it's a bit of an art form. Projects can linger forever as email chains build up, and just as they near common ground they inevitably take a U-turn. Sometimes it isn't clear what's being asked of you, so it's hard to do the job. "Review this and address any red flags" could mean spend an hour reading through it or spend a few weeks addressing key issues with help from outside counsel. And in either case, there's no clear end.

It's your job to create that end. An excellent technique is to politely frame up the issue and put it to rest. You can do this—at any point, even in a long email thread!—by saying something like:

"My understanding from you is the relevant facts are a, b, c and you're asking about x, y, z"; or "… you got an answer already on x and y so you're just asking about z"; or "… you want me to write an email that sounds like your voice that you can copy and paste to answer the customer's question"; and so on.

Then, finish your statement with:

"If that's not right just let me know."

After that, solve the issue you've framed up.

There, you've done it! Instant closure. And not just any closure—a clean record! This is so important because "future you" in 6 or 12 months will likely need to refer back to the advice you gave. If it's unclear what answer you provided and what assumptions you made, you could be forced to redo your work to get back up to speed. A good, clean record makes clear:

- Whose question you're answering;

- What you think the question is;

- What assumptions you're making;

- Your answer in clear terms;

- Any next steps—or the absence thereof (i.e., closure!); and

- An invitation for others to follow up if something isn't right (which hopefully elicits a response like, "Yes, that's right. Thanks for your help answering my question!")

Tip #17: Make outside counsel your partner

Outside counsel can be an essential ally, or they can make your life only marginally easier. You want them to make your life much easier. Even if you're lucky enough to have good outside counsel with tech company experience, you can always improve the working relationship.

Ideally, outside counsel becomes a true partner when you need them. I recommend giving outside counsel context. Remember context is everything? It's true here too. With the right context, outside counsel can solve your problem fully; without context, you'll get an impenetrable memo that's largely inapplicable. Answering the following questions will provide helpful context for outside counsel:

- **Who is involved?** What are their roles? What are the politics?

- **What kind of work product do you want?** An email? A chart? A conversation that's light on the billables?

- **What are the relevant deadlines?** When do you need the work product and what is the rationale?

- **What doesn't matter as much?** What are the areas you don't need help with as much as the areas where their focus will really make an impact?

When you build a strong working relationship with them, outside counsel will feel invested in your projects, commit to your deadlines, provide work that you can immediately utilize, and think strategically to deftly navigate politics, personalities, and roadblocks.

As an aside, I recommend saying a genuine thank you to good outside counsel. It can go a very long way. Many clients treat law firm lawyers like the billable rate is thank you enough. But outside counsel really appreciates feeling like they're part of the team and knowing they're making a difference.

Tip #18: Hire flexible problem-solvers who can communicate

When it comes to hiring, the right match can be idiosyncratic and dependent on business needs and the makeup of the team. Beyond those needs, I recommend hiring for two key skills: problem-solving and communication.

You'll need your direct reports to be able to eventually work independently, and that means navigating all the challenges described in this book. To solve problems, they'll need to be proactive, creative, and able to provide a sound approach in the face of uncertainty.

The second key skill is communication. Communication is so important that I dedicated the entire next Section to it. Good communication is essential for good advice to land smoothly with any audience, and that is a key component to working independently. It's also essential that your direct reports are able to bring you up to speed quickly and clearly.

BECOMING AN EXPERT COMMUNICATOR

In a fast-paced environment, communication is essential. Little things that would not reach outside counsel go wrong daily and require intervention. When communications break down, people get frustrated, issues escalate, and problems go unsolved. In other words, people working together on hard problems under pressure doesn't always go smoothly. For this reason, the best tech company lawyers excel at working with others, de-escalating situations, preventing escalations in the first place, and aligning everyone involved to keep things moving forward.

Tip #19: Context is everything—both receiving and providing

Once again, context is everything, and it's your job to ask the right questions to get the context you need to provide good advice and navigate complicated situations. What led to this question for Legal? What are the stakes? Who is involved, and what should you know about them? Is anyone frustrated and why? What work has been done or is depending on this? Is there a budget for legal work? How does the technology work? The list of contextual questions you might ask is almost endless; these are just a few examples. You will be held accountable for the full benefit of the context even if you were provided with none.

Just as you appreciate colleagues that clearly provide you with the context you need, try to be that colleague to others. I like to use the analogy of city maps with a bright circle and arrow that says "You are here." Try to situate conversations with a similar sense of "You are here" so everyone is on the same page and so next steps are more intuitive.

Tip #20: Start emails and conversations with an implied "because"

On a related note, approach all emails and conversations with an implied "because" as part of what you communicate. At a tech company, the business will always want to know why. That's a good thing. It means you're working with smart, inquisitive colleagues who won't settle for "Legal said so." To be a good partner and communicator, don't issue dictates and don't wait to get asked why. Just assume the question and provide your reasoning. Better yet, tie your reasoning to business goals and not merely the law. For example, you could say something like:

"Great news—we are good to proceed with this vendor without a HIPAA BAA. This is because we worked out a manner to avoid the vendor handling any PHI on our behalf. This creative adjustment allows us to move forward with the vendor even though it is not HIPAA compliant and could not sign a BAA."

On the other hand, if you instead tell your boss or your colleagues "They sent over the thing and it looks good, except for the thing they mentioned last month," they will have no idea who you're talking about, what the "thing" is, or what they mentioned last month. Your boss or colleagues will also have no idea <u>why</u> it looks good or <u>why</u> the thing mentioned last week does not. Which type of communication do you want to provide to others in your workplace?

Just as you should write your emails with an implied "because," you should also have an implied "because" in conversations. In all cases, providing this context to your boss and colleagues will help them make better decisions; and making them look good makes you look good.

Tip #21: Say "I don't know"

It is very important to say "I don't know" when you simply don't know. Bear in mind that "I don't know" is very different from "I won't ever know" or "I can't." But given the nature of tech company work, there is a lot you won't know on the spot. Don't lose credibility by taking a wild swing you have to walk back later. And definitely don't deflect or confuse the conversation like a White House press secretary or an NFL coach at a post-game press conference. If you don't know, just say so. Then make sure you ask the right question for context and go work on finding an answer.

Tip #22: Analogies are so useful

Communication is about clarity and alignment between all parties. Analogies are a terrific shortcut for distilling a complex concept into something simple and accessible, and for developing a shared understanding.

During my time working with tech companies in the digital health space, lawyers frequently consider real-world activities as an analogy for how things should work online. For example:

- How do doctor's offices ask if your insurance has changed?

- How do doctors get a patient's consent to send unencrypted emails?

- How do doctors present patients with a Notice of Privacy Practices?
- Ultimately, how do we replicate these activities online?

Some of my favorite analogies have involved more abstract concepts. A good analogy makes perfect sense to everyone involved even if it isn't immediately obvious to others. The "inside baseball" feeling of an analogy creates a simplified and common vernacular for complex concepts. Here are a few effective analogies I've used in the past:

- Different colored cows representing different types of data sharing.
  - *Why this is helpful*: When a new data sharing request comes in, you can ask if it fits in a known and previously evaluated category (e.g. "a brown cow") or is different and in need of a new analysis (e.g., "a white cow").
- An international space station (ISS) representing multiple products with common legal terms.
  - *Why this is helpful*: When a new product is in development you can ask whether it will have the same universal legal terms as existing products (i.e., part of the ISS) or will it need its own unique terms (i.e., outside of the ISS).

- Even chopping heads off of dolls representing removing all personally identifiable information from a data set.

  › *Why this is helpful*: This visual representation for de-identifying data gets a bit more colorful than I'll spell out here, but suffice it to say it was vivid and everyone got it.

Analogies and illustrations are also humanizing (notwithstanding the slightly graphic doll analogy). They allow you to use humor to show you're not just a robotic lawyer. For example, I got really excited when I got to use the phrase "August and Everything After" to describe records of privacy training completions that started in August. Anyone who listened to the Counting Crows in the 1990s took a collective moment to reminisce.

Tip #23: Following up is key

I covered the importance of following up in Tip #4: "Work management is essential." It is so important for good communication that I'll repeat it here. Good communication means checking in to see whether your advice is still needed, your advice has been taken, any updates have occurred, or just if you can help in a new way. Follow-up also helps you identify earlier on if someone is getting frustrated so you can help de-escalate the situation. Once again, I suggest setting up a reminder to yourself—using the system of your choice—immediately after a meeting or sending an email that will require follow up. This is often necessary to keep things on track and to stay aligned with your colleagues. Good advice that doesn't get implemented or that grows stale loses its value.

WORKING WITH OTHER TEAMS

This Section offers an introduction to key tech company departments you're likely to encounter on the job. The goal is to help familiarize you with teams that lawyers work with and give you a sense of their roles and perspectives.

If you haven't worked at a tech company where you interact closely with colleagues across the business, you may be unfamiliar with how the other departments work. When you are a lawyer at a firm or even a large, established corporation, you may never meet the person on the other end of the phone line. You may not even know what department the client works for, and you are likely unfamiliar with the political pressures within their organization.

As a result, you won't necessarily provide advice within

the context of those politics. In fact, you might not even concern yourself with implementation once you have dispensed advice on how to comply with the law. But that's all very different at a tech company.

Tip #24: How to be a good partner to the business

A central theme of this book is that relationships dictate success, and that you need more than legal skills to be a good partner to the business. Hallmarks of a good partner include:

- **Communicate clearly and simply about legal concepts**. Be proactive in explaining "why" (see Tip #20: "Start emails and conversations with an implied 'because'").

- **Be business-friendly**. Genuinely try to understand the business objective, product, technical material, engineering workflows, analytics tools, and complicated advertising technology (AdTech). Consider the implications of legal decisions on other teams' workloads and on customers (see Tip #33: "Never forget the customers").

- **Have an effective and realistic assessment of risk**. Think broadly about risks, including both their probability and potential harm, consider non-legal risks, and think creatively about how to address them. (See Tip #7: "Get comfortable managing risk").

- **Be enjoyable to work with.** Show enthusiasm. Have a sense of humor. Make references to your favorite band from the nineties when you have the opportunity.

- **Have an ethical compass and a respect for users.** It's the right thing to do and it rubs off on others.

- **Proactively monitor the legal landscape.** Bring the business practical guidance on how to respond. Provide trainings and reminders, and keep policies updated.

- **Handle inevitable escalations calmly and professionally.** Manage the situation carefully, with problem-solving and teamwork, to advance the conversation and help leadership make an informed decision.

- **Help defend the product or business decisions to customers and users.** Be firm but reasonable in that process. Always make sure the consumer voice is heard.

Practices like these are essential to being a good partner to the business and make a difference no matter what team you're working with.

Tip #25: Working with the product team

The product team is the team developing the next futuristic product and ensuring that the current product evolves to best serve the customer and users. Your role is to help the product team build new products and product updates on time while remaining compliant with laws, protecting intellectual property, getting paid, and so on. You want to work with the product team early and often so things get built right the first time. This can be especially rewarding work, and I'd go so far as to say if you don't like working with the product team, this is probably not the right job for you, or you're working with the wrong company.

As you're building a good working relationship with the product team, it helps to be aware of key lingo like "features," "verticals," and "horizontals." Products consist of several features, and if the product is large enough (think Facebook) it will have product teams dedicated to individual features (think newsfeed, messages, marketplace, stories, etc.) Each product and its features is a "vertical," while "horizontals" are lateral, supporting products that serve multiple verticals. Examples of a horizontal include identity management/ authentication, analytics, reporting to customers, and experience design. Depending on the size of your company and your level of specialization (e.g., privacy, IP counsel, employment counsel), you may work with multiple products or you may be dedicated to a particular product.

The product team has a roadmap for launching products and features, and that roadmap drives their functions. Your job is to understand their vision and help them achieve that vision while doing your best to adhere to the roadmap. If possible, you also want to integrate your legal advice effectively into their workflow. Emails and meetings may be sufficient for some teams, but if you can integrate your advice directly into tools of the product team, such as demos, mocks, product requirements documents (PRDs), and project management tickets, go for it. The product team will appreciate it, and your advice is most likely to get read and implemented when it's front and center.

Tip #26: Working with the engineering team

Engineering is very likely home to some of the company's key talent. Depending on the company, engineers may even be considered the "heroes." That's not always the case; maybe the company provides medical care, backed by technology, and your nurses and doctors are revered, or maybe you have the best design team in town. But at a tech company, everything runs on technology—so your engineers are always indispensable.

They probably know it too, and larger companies would love to steal engineering talent away. This helps explain some of the more idiosyncratic elements of offices such as fun conference room names, Taco Bell Fridays, and Irreverent T-Shirts Everydays. So, enjoy the free lunch, snack bar, casual attire, ping pong table, pop-a-shot, or whatever else your tech company offers to lure top engineering talent. This ain't happening at big law firms or the government.

In short, be grateful for engineers and try to understand them. As an admittedly vast generalization, engineers tend to think in black and white. Coding works with "If/Then" statements, not "If/Maybe." The technology either works or it doesn't, and engineers tend to look for similarly clear-cut advice.

So how can you work well with engineering?

- **Be genuinely curious to understand the tech.** Do an internet search, chat about it over lunch, and don't be intimidated. If someone is a good teacher on the engineering team, ask them to walk you through it on a whiteboard.

- **But also be judicious.** Every moment spent teaching you how the integration environment or logical separation of data works is time away from the current engineering sprint. So part of being a good tech company lawyer is having the savvy to know when to dig deeper in order to provide the right advice and when to go learn from a YouTube video or wait to bring up questions at the next happy hour.

- **Be curious about how Agile engineering development works so you understand the engineering workflow.** Know how sprints, epics, and stories work so you understand their timing and prioritization. Agile is a method of product development consisting of short (e.g., three-week) "sprints" to build only the immediate next step, with flexibility to pivot at any time. This contrasts with more traditional waterfall engineering design which starts with the end goal and plans all sequential steps to get there. "Epics" and their smaller component, "stories," are names for projects as divided into their parts. The size of a project can be measured in "story points" which ties to engineering work hours required. All of this information tells you how to work with engineering—for instance, whether new ideas from Legal can get implemented in the current sprint or need to wait for a future sprint.

- **Work with the ticketing system for assigning and tracking engineering work.** If possible, provide feedback in the engineering team's workflow. As with the product team, the engineering team will appreciate it, and your advice is most likely to get read and implemented when it's front and center.

- **Give clear, black-and-white advice wherever possible.** Where necessary, gently explain areas where ambiguity can help you get the engineering team where they want to go.

- **Do not underestimate how much work everything takes.** Nothing in engineering is easy, time is money, and it all has to be QA'd.

Tip #27: Working with the marketing team

The marketing team's goal is to create positive brand awareness and get the product in the hands of as many customers and users as possible. How do they do that? Any way they can, including:

- Emails sent by the company
- Emails sent by customers
- Push notifications
- Cookies, internet advertising, and related AdTech
- Texts
- Mailers
- Billboards
- Person spinning a sign
- Incentives ($5 if you sign up)
- Festivals
- Sweepstakes
- Brand ambassadors
- Conference booths
- And so on.

Marketing is very attuned to their budget and ROI, and the diversity of their initiatives can be deceptively complicated. Also, marketing professionals do not necessarily have technical or legal backgrounds, and they won't always understand how the latest internet advertising and cookies work at a granular level. This can present unexpected challenges for you and the legal department—for example, the marketing team may not know what identifiers are shared with third parties or whether a sweepstakes they're proposing implicates state laws around lotteries. So, there are rocks to look under with marketing initiatives, and your goal is to look under those rocks while steadfastly supporting the campaign's objectives, on budget, and with enthusiasm!

Tip #28: Working with account management and support

Every product or feature is developed in the context of users and/or customers. Users and customers are not shy about what they like or don't like. Especially in the world of tech, feedback can be provided and shared instantaneously and widely. To manage these relationships, tech companies hire account managers focused on customers and support teams focused on handling user calls and emails.

These same teams field legal concerns from users and customers. Accordingly, there is a symbiotic relationship between Legal and account management and support. You'll work alongside each other to address thorny legal questions that come up.

Train them on fielding standard legal questions, give them template responses, and let them know when to escalate questions to the legal team. In this way, they can help shield you from day-to-day questions, and you can help them manage the more challenging/unusual questions. And ask them for context about key customers, contracts up for renewal or out to bid, difficult customer personalities, etc. By understanding the customers and users, you'll be positioned to give better advice to other teams (as described in Tip #33: "Never forget the customers" and Tip #34: "Never forget the users or society").

Tip #29: Working with other teams

There are of course other teams that you will work with. Because you will work them less frequently (but still regularly), I'll address some of them more briefly here.

- **Security.** You can't be an in-house tech lawyer without thinking about security. First of all, like the legal team, the security team is in the business of protecting the company. You will do well to make Security a partner in compliance, contract negotiation, audits, and security certifications like SOC-2 and HITRUST CSF. Team with them on security-related contracts such as security agreements. Also, a security problem can generate economic and legal risk, loss of trust and subsequent loss of customers, and harm to users. Legal risk in particular can take the form of contractual breaches, lawsuits, violations of Service Level Agreements (SLAs) with customers, breach reporting requirements under state, federal, or ex-US laws, and FTC violations for unfair or deceptive practices. So, it pays to work closely with Security and bring them in if they aren't already involved in a project.

- **Sales & Business Development (BD).** First and foremost, Sales and BD want you to help get the deal done, like right now or maybe yesterday. Typically, revenue (not to mention Sales and BD team bonuses) depends on contracts getting signed quickly. You'll want to align on the right contract language, which template you'll use, who has negotiation responsibilities, and where the company is willing to compromise versus insisting on holding the line. And you'll want to have each other's back: Legal can do this with responsiveness and efficient contractual review; Sales and BD can do this by giving Legal as much notice of timing and expectations as possible. Sales and BD also want to know what they can promise to potential customers and partners. They will look to you to help answer questions and Requests for Proposals (RFPs) from potential customers, and they will team with you on contract negotiations. They're not looking for a memo, but rather a clean, clear, user-friendly answer that will reassure the customer.

- **Data/Analytics.** The data team will want to manipulate data, de-identify it, aggregate it, share it, and publish it—all of which will require legal/privacy input on what's permissible under contracts and applicable laws. Like AdTech, this is another area where you need to understand some very technical details and to ask for that context.

- **HR.** HR will work with Legal primarily on employment matters, such as offer letters, non-competes, ownership of inventions, separations, sanctions, codes of conduct, and so on. There is a symbiotic relationship here and some tough decisions to be made together. Also, given the overlap between Legal and HR, if your HR team isn't organized, the legal team may find itself influencing/improving or even taking on HR practices.

- **Experience design.** You'll work with designers to integrate legal terms into product design. Enjoy working with creative thinkers and look for compromises, but remember that white font on a white background does not make for an effective—or legally valid—notice.

- **Finance/Procurement.** Finance and procurement can each be an excellent partner when reviewing vendors. Finance needs to review budgets for vendors and Procurement has its own protocols, so you can and should have each other's backs to make sure each team has reviewed and approved the vendor.

Tip #30: To the non-lawyers: Working with Legal

If you work at a tech company and you stole this book off your legal colleague's desk or picked it up as a gift, I hope it helps capture what to expect from a good tech company lawyer. I also have a few suggestions for how you can work best with the legal team:

- **Bring the lawyers in early.** Planning and directional steering with the legal team will save time later.

- **Provide context.** Lawyers—especially those who have read this book—are hungry for context to help them provide the most useful advice.

- **Leave the legal conclusions to the lawyers.** By all means, share all facts you think are relevant, but you can—and should—let the lawyers characterize things in the eyes of the law.

- **Ask more of your lawyers.** You can expect your legal team to be an active partner in furthering business objectives, meeting deadlines, representing the brand, and thinking strategically, all while protecting the company.

- **Do you want a "yes" or a "no"?** Good lawyers will assume you want to get to "yes," but sometimes the business team wants the lawyers to say "no"—e.g., to a customer or even to another team. Within reason, lawyers can help you make an argument that aligns with your goals. So, let the legal team know where you ideally want to land the plane.

THINGS YOU SHOULD KNOW WELL

Even if you have strong legal skills, give good advice, and work well with other teams, it will set you apart if you know a few essential things well: the products, the business and industry, the customers, and the users. This might seem obvious, but it's not a given because knowing each of these well takes homework. Putting in the effort is well worth it.

Tip #31: Know the product(s)

It is essential that you know your company's products well. I can't stress this enough. As a tech company lawyer, you may be surprised to find that not everyone on your legal team knows the product cold. In fact, even product and engineering teams may only know the details of the particular product feature they're working on.

A FEW TIPS TO DEVELOP STRONG PRODUCT KNOWLEDGE

- Use the product regularly, especially after version updates or feature releases.

- Look up any technical terms you're not familiar with in product summaries or legal agreements.

- Watch or join product team meetings. If you're not invited, ask! Most business teams are thrilled to have a lawyer who is so interested in what they're building.

- Talk to people at lunch and in the halls. Learn about what they're up to.

- If there are "release notes" that summarize product updates, get on the distribution list and review them.

Be the exception to the rule. Use the product. Talk about the product. Have opinions on the product and where it's going next. Tech companies call this "eating your own dog food" or "drinking your own champagne." This simple act demonstrates you're a team player. Better still, it will allow you to provide better legal and business advice. For example, if you work with multiple product teams, your lateral knowledge may be a unique strength in the organization. I described the value of using data to make decisions in Tip #6: "Use data for decisions"; sometimes, the most critical data is an understanding of how the product actually works.

Tip #32: Know the business and the industry

It's also essential to know the business and the industry. What is the business's strategy and how is it tracking? What are its priorities for the year, the quarter, or even the month? Where has there been turnover? Where are there hiring needs? Is revenue growing on pace? What is the company's NPS?

Product development takes place in the context of the business. Again, if you work with a lot of business teams, you may have a unique ability to see trends across the business. If you pay attention, you'll understand the politics, and you'll know how to prioritize.

A FEW TIPS TO DEVELOP STRONG COMPANY AND INDUSTRY KNOWLEDGE

- Attend all company "All Hands" meetings, town halls, or other high-level updates.

- Set a Google Alert for the company—and possibly for its C-suite and competitors.

- Read industry press and listen to podcasts on industry trends or featuring leaders at your company. Do likewise with blogs, books, YouTube, or other media. Follow competitors on LinkedIn.

- Consider attending an industry conference on non-legal topics relevant to your work.

- Consider using competitor products to better understand the marketplace.

- If your company has personnel dedicated to competitive intelligence, read what they produce and ask your way onto their distribution list.

Likewise, the business takes place in the context of the industry. Competition can dictate priorities and put pressure on certain product features to stay ahead or keep up with the marketplace. Arm yourself with this information and you'll be better able to advise the business.

Tip #33: Never forget the customers

If your tech company has business customers, then it's also essential to keep them in mind. Do you know your company's top 20 customers in terms of annual revenue? That context will influence how everyone responds to a particular customer's request, and you should have that context as well.

Customers can make all kinds of demands, and often they will want to change legal terms or user consents. One of the great debates for a tech company is whether to customize the product and legal terms for large or demanding customers. It requires all kinds of work, like keeping track of customer restrictions when you add new features. But for the right amount of revenue or a customer that makes your reputation, it's worthwhile. The answer for your organization depends on many factors and leverage, but your job is to understand the organization's stance on customization. And if customizations will impact legal terms and rights, it's your job to keep track of them.

CUSTOMER DEMANDS ARE A GOOD EXAMPLE OF NON-LEGAL RISK

In Tip #7: "Get comfortable managing risk," I discussed the importance of speaking in terms of non-legal risk. Dealing with customers provides a perfect example. I've had multiple discussions about the tension between legal terms (lawyers want to make them clear and unmissable!) and user experience (designers want to make it seamless and legal terms unobtrusive!) that have been settled by considering the demands of customers. If key or noisy customers are likely to express concerns with a particular design, that will almost surely be more compelling than a discussion of Circuit splits regarding electronic signatures or binding terms of service.

Tip #34: Never forget the users or society

This may be the cheesiest piece of advice, but I stand by it. As technology advances, remembering users and society is more important than ever. Amazon leaves an empty chair in each meeting to represent the customer. For a time, my screen saver said "Put the users first" to remind myself and others when they walked by.

Think about the user experience that results from decisions you make. Is a "dark pattern" taking shape (even accidentally), will users be confused, and is this what they really want? Product developers may mean well but can be so close to what they're building that they make incorrect assumptions about what users will understand.

How do you know if something is unclear? Once again, if at all possible, get the data. See if users are tripping up on a particular screen or failing to take advantage of certain features. The data tells the story and can validate your hunch.

As for society, critiques of tech companies are well known, including privacy, government surveillance, culture, diversity, discrimination, social justice, false information, and so on. To name a few critical books for further reading, see *Uncanny Valley* by Anna Wiener, *Weapons of Math Destruction* by Cathy O'Neil, and *Brotopia* by Emily Chang, or watch *The Social Dilemma* or *Citizenfour*.

That's not to scare you away. Rather, lawyers are well positioned to articulate what's in society's best interest. Consider it part of the role.

OFFICE LIFE DURING CORONAVIRUS AND AFTER

Most of the advice in this book is relevant regardless of the office. Still, there are strategies to optimize the office context, whether you're working from home or in an open-office plan of the future. In this Section, I discuss how to make the most of remote work (during coronavirus and after) and a likely eventual return to an open office plan. The work of navigating each environment is not unique to lawyers, but it is important to make the most of your situation because the expectations—e.g., giving good advice and working well with other teams—remain constant.

Tip #35: Advice on working remotely

These days, you can't talk about work without talking about working remotely due to coronavirus. That will not always be the case, but remote work will likely remain a larger part of work life. Working at home has challenges that are well-known to us all: distractions, interruptions, fewer informal interactions, difficulty turning work off, isolation, and so on. As a tech company lawyer, you may have certain advantages. You may be used to working from home due to a permissive remote work culture, and you may benefit from a tech-friendly workplace that is well suited for remote work. Even so, there are critical challenges that need to be addressed when it comes to working with other teams and providing effective advice remotely.

- **Get plugged into workflows.** The only way you can give good advice is to be in the conversation. If you spent years at your company before coronavirus, this may come easily at first, but stay vigilant because it can wear off. If you're newer to your company, or even onboarded during the pandemic, you really need to work at it. If you have any calls that ask for a volunteer, raise your hand. Follow up with people you meet on calls and make sure you're aligned on next steps. Make sure you know key contacts from the teams you work with and reach out to them regularly to follow up on projects.

Ask those contacts if there are meetings you should join, and then show up.

- **Ask "How can I help you?"** More than ever, a can-do attitude is essential. And the best way to demonstrate that attitude is to ask how you can help. Ask to be a special guest at other teams' meetings, prepare a short presentation on an issue facing their teams and how you propose to solve it, and offer to assist. I also recommend occasional "How can I help you?" meetings with key contacts from other teams. Without a set agenda, let others tell you what they're working on—you will naturally spot issues and be able to offer assistance. Just like that, you'll be part of their workflow and you'll start on the right foot because you offered to solve their problem.

- **Meet others working from home for coffee.** Just because you're working from home doesn't mean you can't be social. Depending on your comfort level, and especially when coronavirus is under control, you can still meet up with colleagues when you're both working from home. Naturally, you have to live nearby, but if you do, consider getting together outside the office to team up in person.

Tip #36: Advice on a return to an open floor plan

Of course, there's no guarantee that we will return to an open floor plan, or even offices, but we're all optimistic that coronavirus vaccines and treatments will lead us back into shared office space. Due to its cost effectiveness, a return to some sort of open floor plan is likely in a post-coronavirus world, though perhaps with new spins like a remote-first workforce and hotel style desks reserved for the day. Should you find yourself making the transition from a law firm office or from home to an open-floor plan, here's how to make the most of it.

- **Position yourself in space to connect with the business.** If you have a choice, you want your desk to be physically close to where the product, engineering, marketing, etc. teams sit and where their daily flows take them. That way, you can maximize opportunities to solve problems on the fly and feel like you're part of their workflow.

- **Book conference rooms ahead of time.** At the same time, lawyers need a private space to talk about sensitive or confidential information. Shared conference rooms are frequently booked, so plan ahead. If your legal team is large enough, consider lobbying for a dedicated conference room for the legal team. Plan for calls to run over, and have a backup plan. I've had to continue some of my most important calls sitting on the floor of a storage room hoping my cell phone wouldn't run out of battery (bring a battery pack!)

- **Take advantage of the whole office.** The layout of the office space itself can offer plenty of opportunities to build rapport with other teams. Spend time in the kitchen, eat lunch with other teams, play games in the office, etc. At Rally Health, we had a thriving ping pong culture, so I played my share of matches during the day and after hours. Eventually, I developed a reputation (I'm a former tennis player), and many in the company knew me from ping pong before we worked together. That camaraderie really helped when we eventually teamed up on projects.

- **Be willing to answer questions on the fly.** When you get drop-by questions, have fun with the challenge. Grab a whiteboard and work on it. See how much you can answer off the cuff. Of course, some questions require a deeper dive, so know when to say you'll get back to them. Be good to your word and follow up.

- **Find a space to do heady, intellectual work.** You will also need time away from distractions to do your most challenging work. So, while I recommend you generally be present and available, I also recommend you find a space that allows you to concentrate (e.g., work from home or a coffee shop) when you really need to focus.

- **Smile**. Be approachable. Wear a smile. Make a (work appropriate) joke. Know everyone's name. These small efforts can help you become a trusted partner.

There are unique joys and challenges of working as a tech company lawyer, and the open office plan is one of them. Armed with the techniques in this book, and of course your substantive legal training and background, you should be ready to thrive.

CONCLUSION

Tech company legal work is fast paced and high stakes. The law is complicated and often trails the pace of technology. It's a challenging combination. But the work of a tech company lawyer is deeply rewarding. It requires teamwork, flexibility, sound judgment, work management, expert communication, and a deep investment in products and their users. It will make you a better lawyer and prepare you for other roles in your career, legal or otherwise. I hope the messages I've shared in this book help you achieve your goals and you become an effective and thoughtful tech company lawyer.

CONCLUSION

AMAZON REVIEWS
AND CONTACTING ME

Thank you for reading this book. I hope it has been helpful to you! If you enjoyed or benefited from it, you can help me by leaving an honest review on Amazon. It takes just a minute and you don't need to use your real name if you prefer. Every review makes a difference, so thank you!

Also, please reach out! You can visit **davidsclar.com** and send me a note there or email me at **techlawyerdave@gmail.com**. I'd love to hear from you.

Sincerely,
David

Made in the USA
Las Vegas, NV
04 January 2024

83854365R00052